MW00700412

Terrific Tunes for Two

7 Exciting Duets for Elementary to Late Elementary Pianists

Martha Mier

Foreword

Something magical occurs when piano students share their music through ensemble playing! Playing duets with friends or family members is an exciting and fun aspect of piano study.

The seven duets in *Terrific Tunes for Two*, Book 1 will encourage the elementary piano student to play with imagination. Both the primo and secondo parts are written at an equal level of difficulty.

It is my sincere hope that these duets will provide much pleasure and entertainment for both the performers and the audience. So find a duet partner and have a terrific time sharing music!

Cover art: Steve Curtis

Alfred

The Old Rocking Chair

Secondo

Gently

Both hands one octave lower than written

Martha Mier

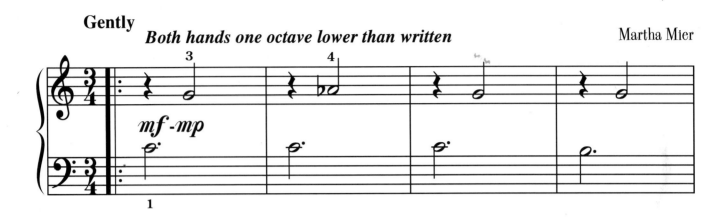

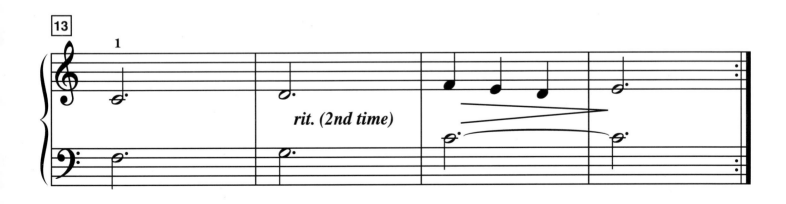

The Old Rocking Chair

Primo

Gently

2nd time both hands one octave higher than written

Martha Mier

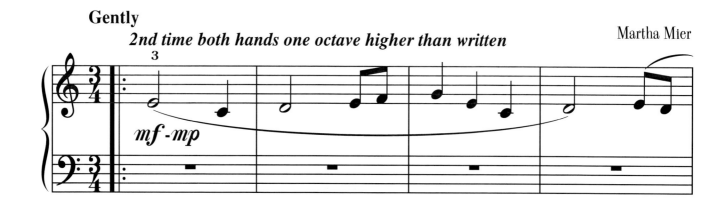

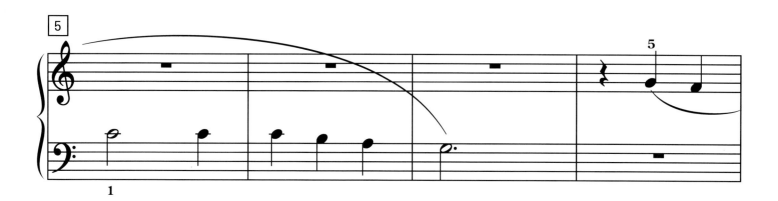

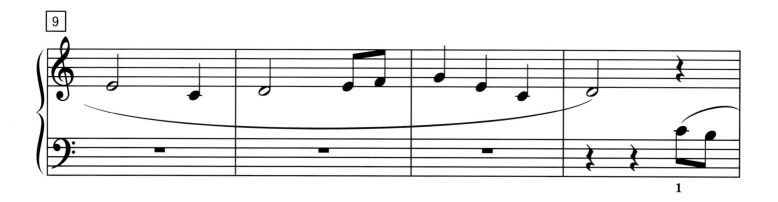

Dandelion Waltz

Secondo

Martha Mier

Cheerfully
RH one octave lower than written

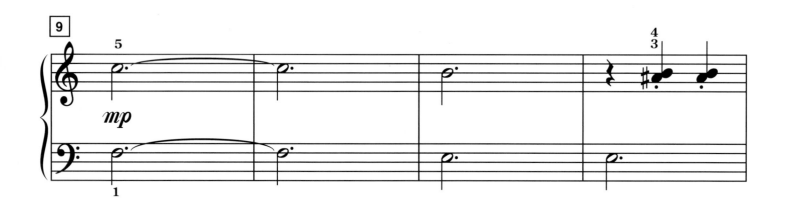

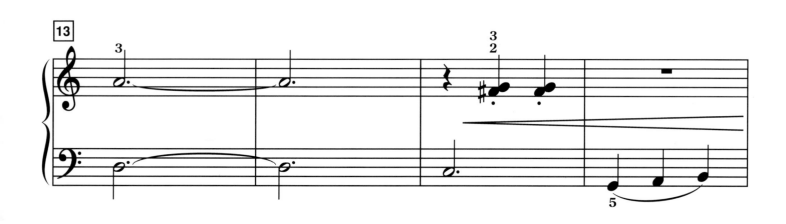

Dandelion Waltz

Primo

Cheerfully

Both hands one octave higher than written

Martha Mier

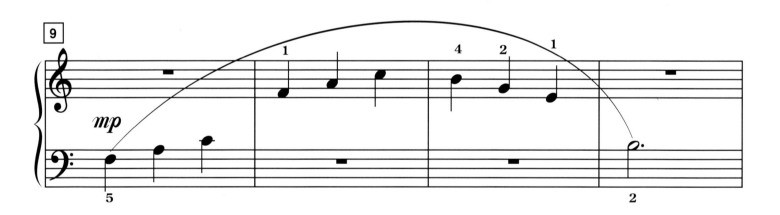

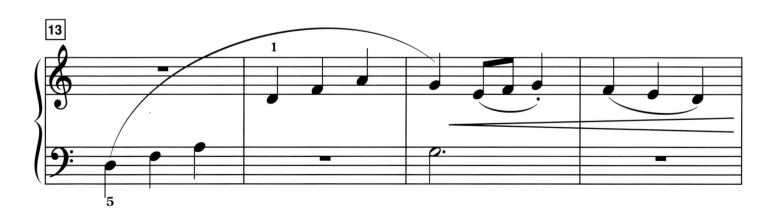

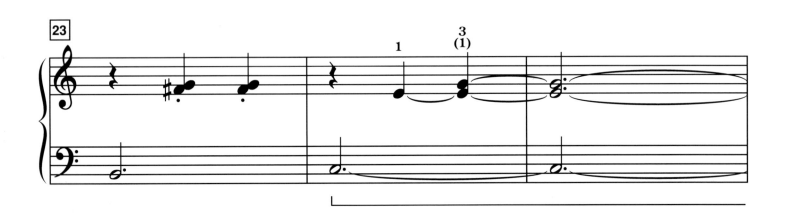

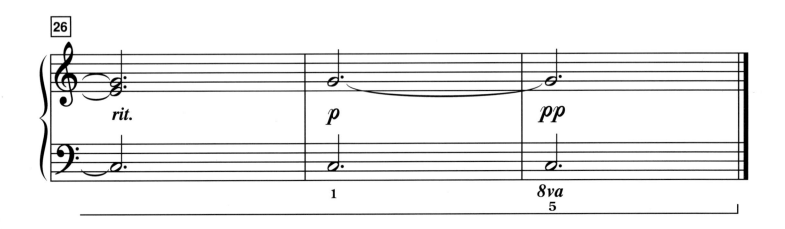

Primo

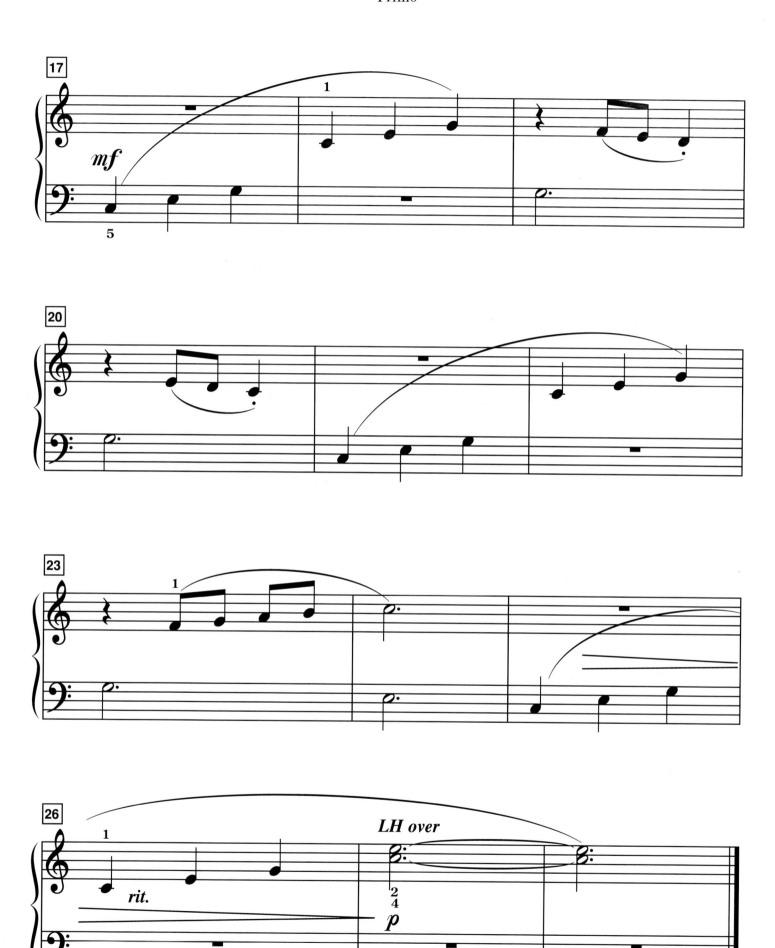

Evening Prayer

Secondo

Quietly

Both hands one octave lower than written

Martha Mier

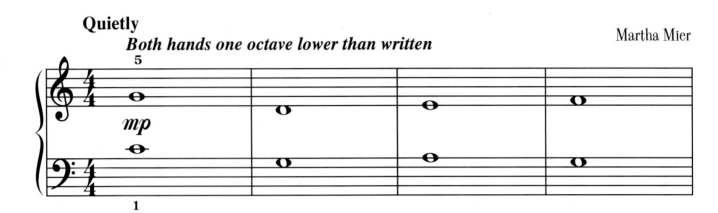

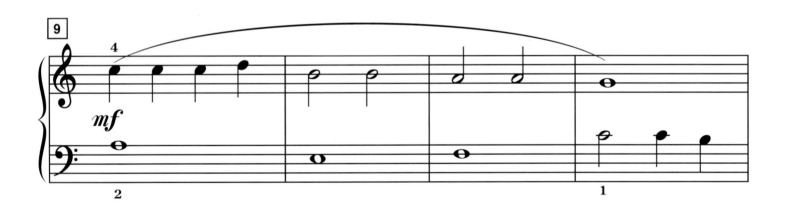

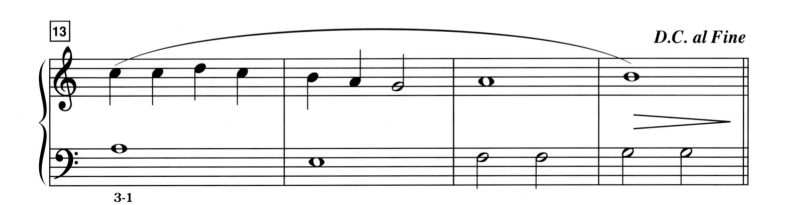

Evening Prayer

Primo

Martha Mier

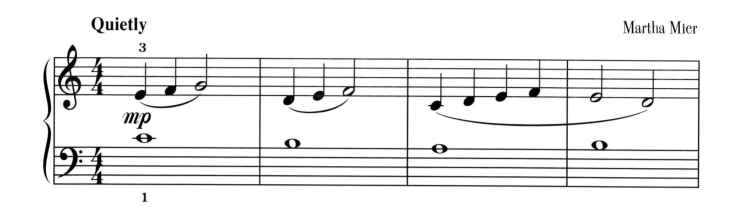

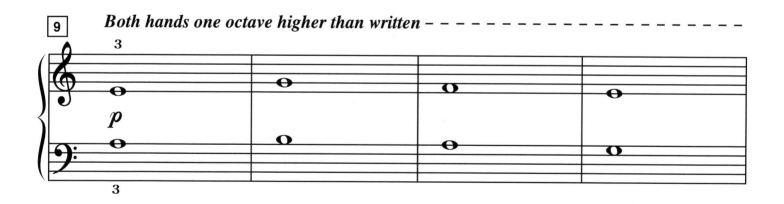

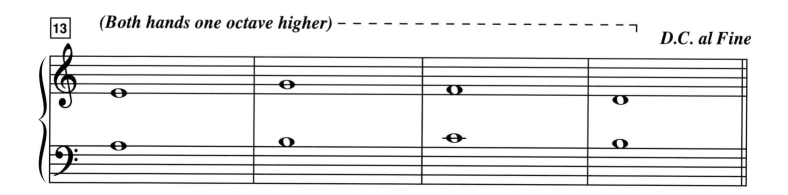

First Waltz

Secondo

Happily

Both hands one octave lower than written

Martha Mier

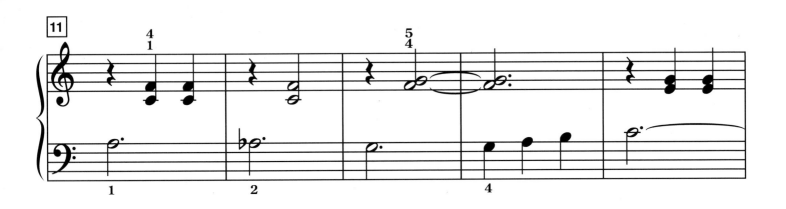

First Waltz

Primo

Happily
Both hands one octave higher than written

Martha Mier

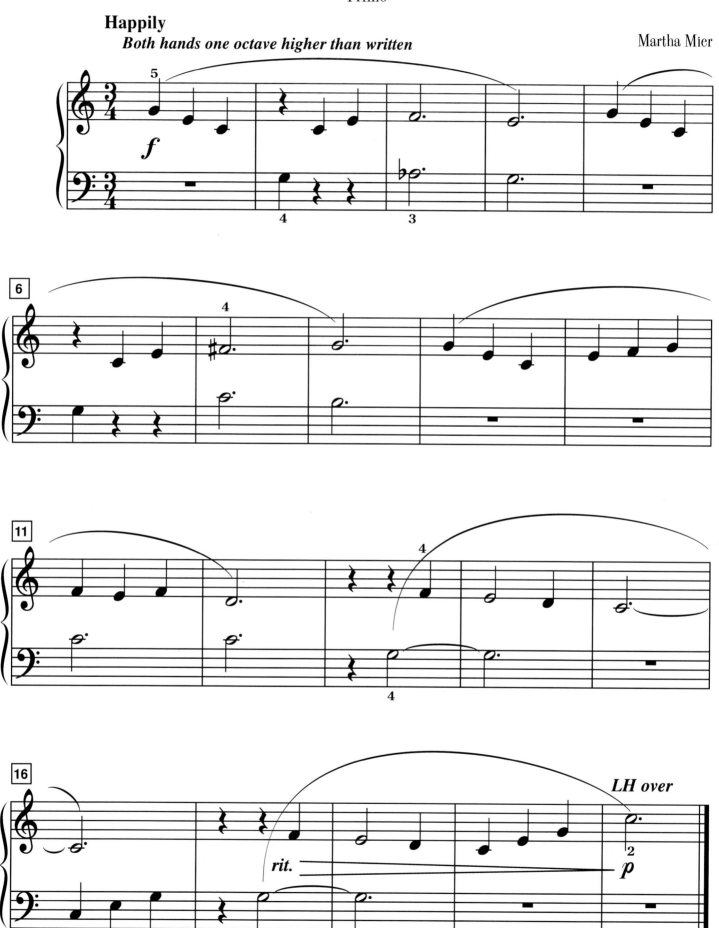

Shoe Shinin' Blues

Secondo

Lazily

Both hands one octave lower than written

Martha Mier

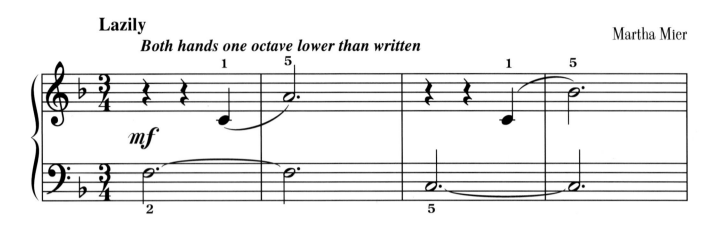

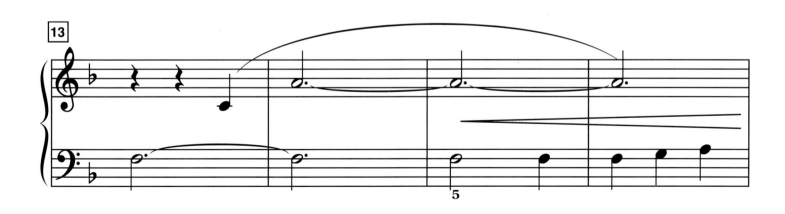

Shoe Shinin' Blues

Primo

Both hands one octave higher than written

Martha Mier

Secondo

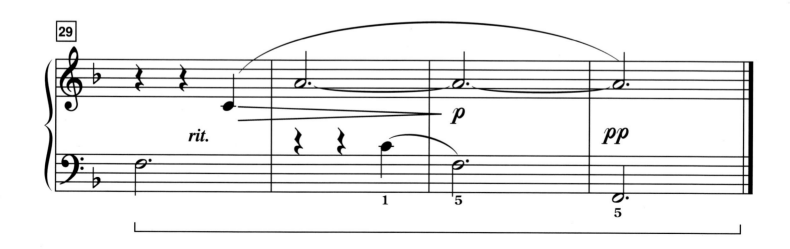

Primo

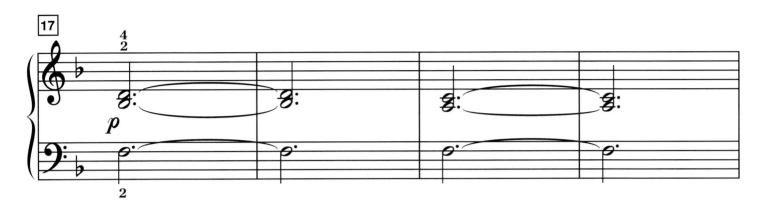

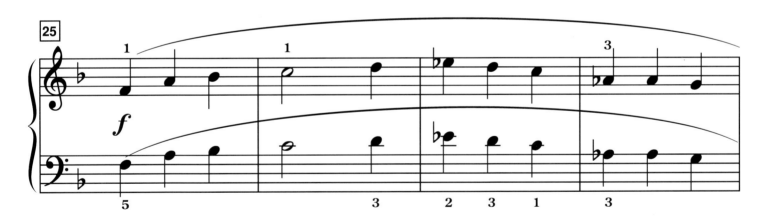

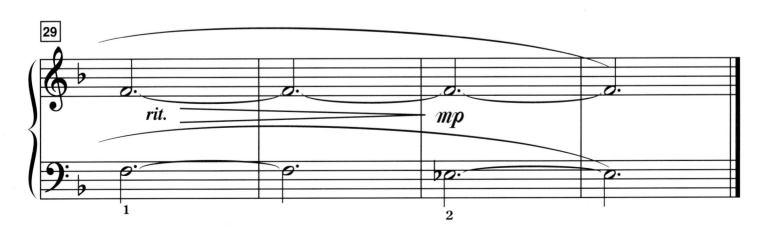

Moonlight Stillness

Secondo

Unhurried

RH one octave lower than written

Martha Mier

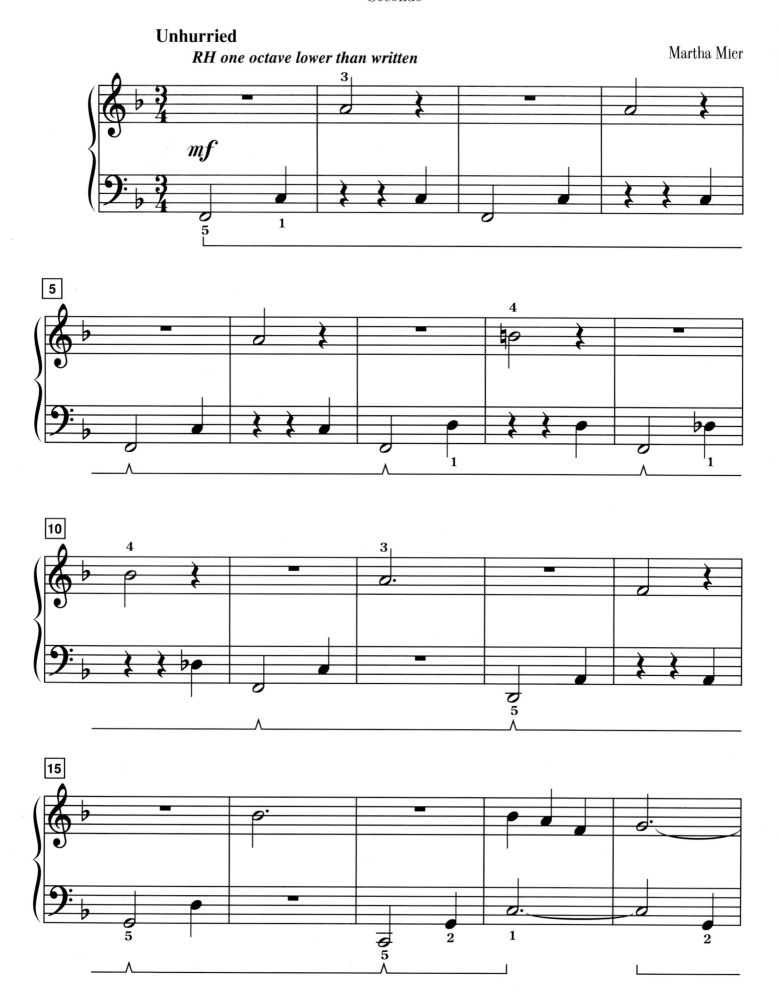

Moonlight Stillness

Primo

Martha Mier

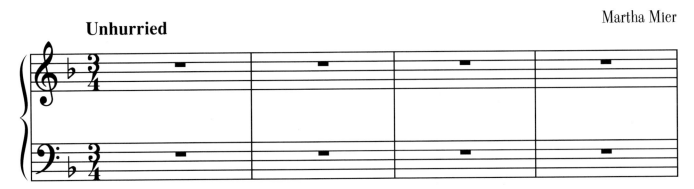

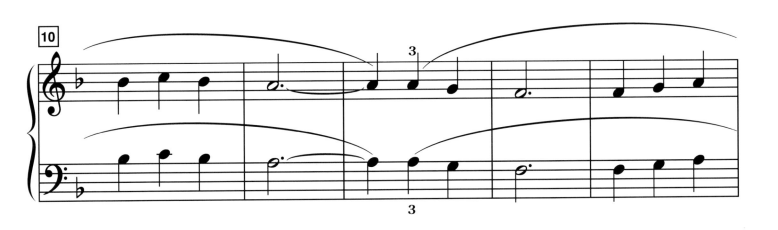

Secondo

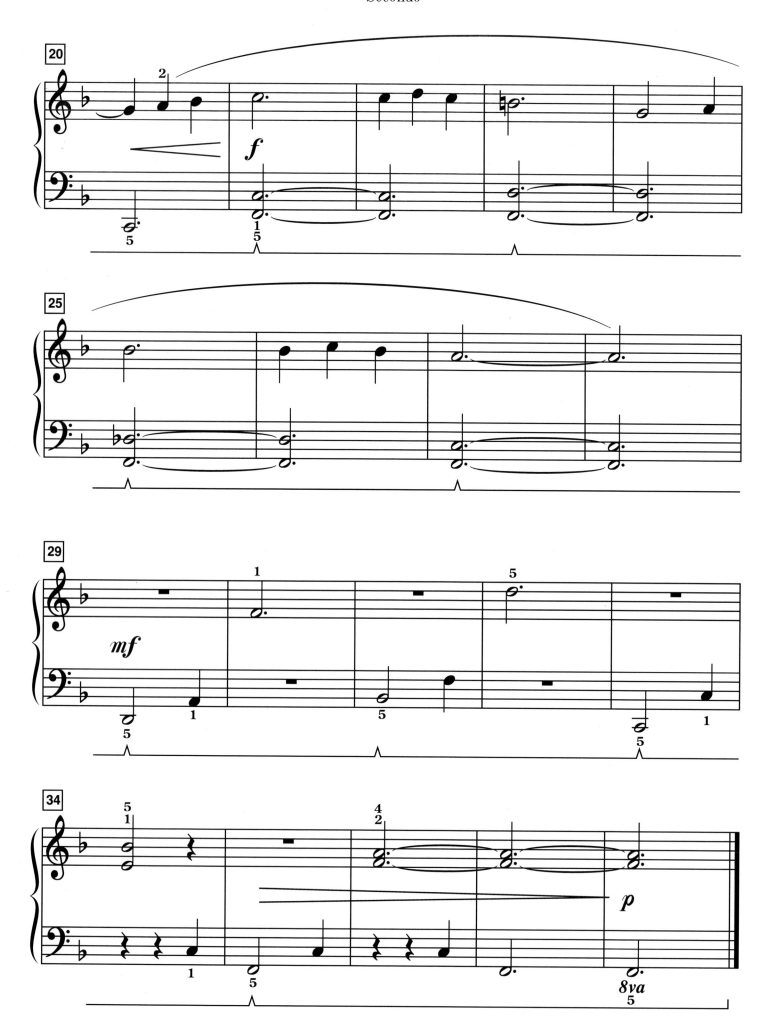

Primo

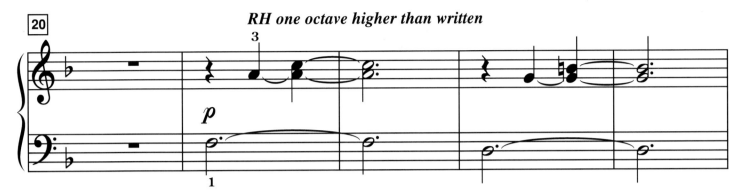

RH one octave higher than written

LH two octaves higher than written

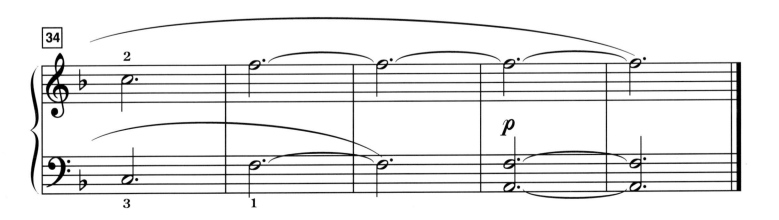

Red Rooster Strut

Secondo

Jauntily

Martha Mier

Both hands one octave lower than written

Red Rooster Strut

Primo

Jauntily

Martha Mier

LH one octave higher than written

Secondo

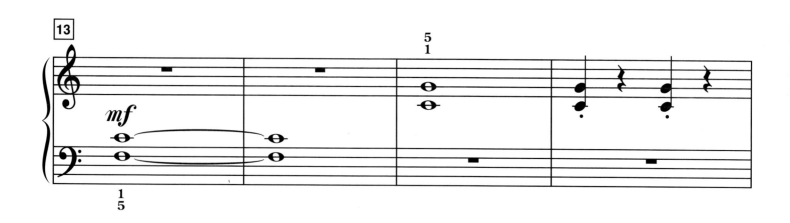

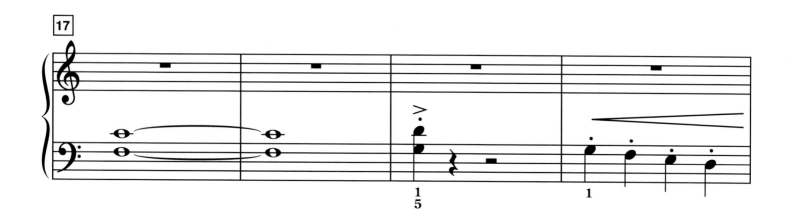

Primo

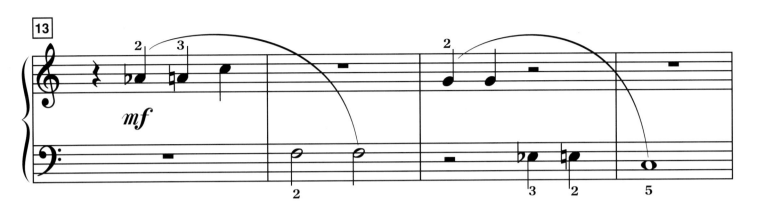

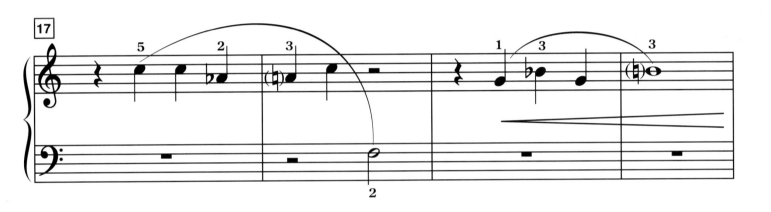

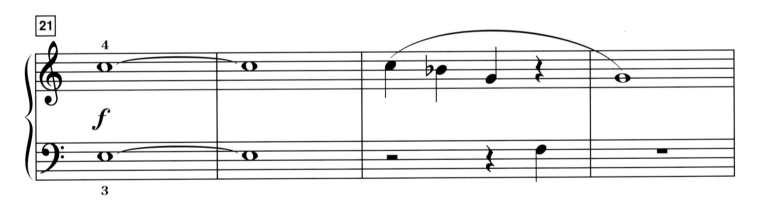